We Like

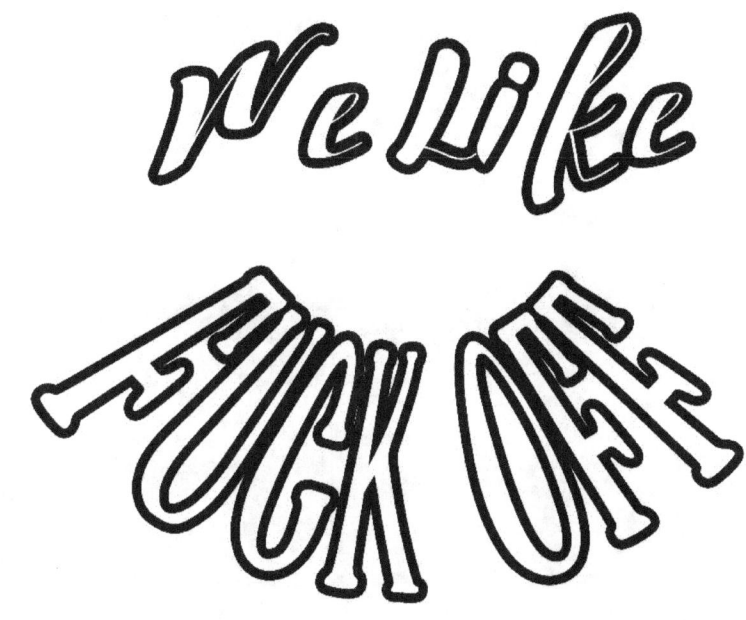

FUCK OFF

Brilliant Swear Word To Color

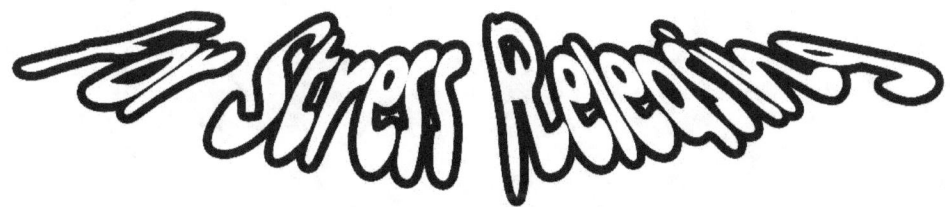

For Stress Releasing

Bear Smit kbet

Happy Coloring!

☐

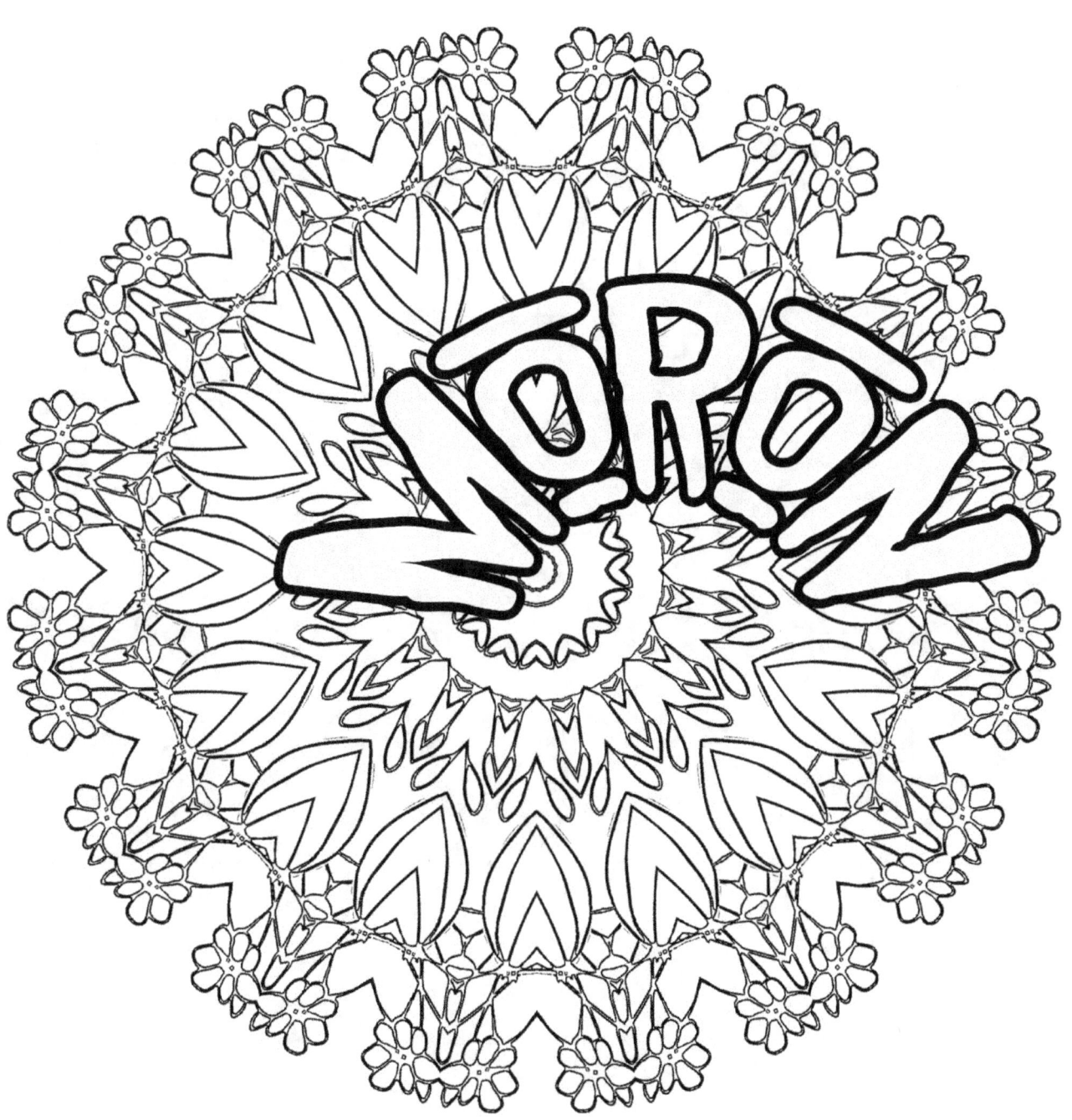

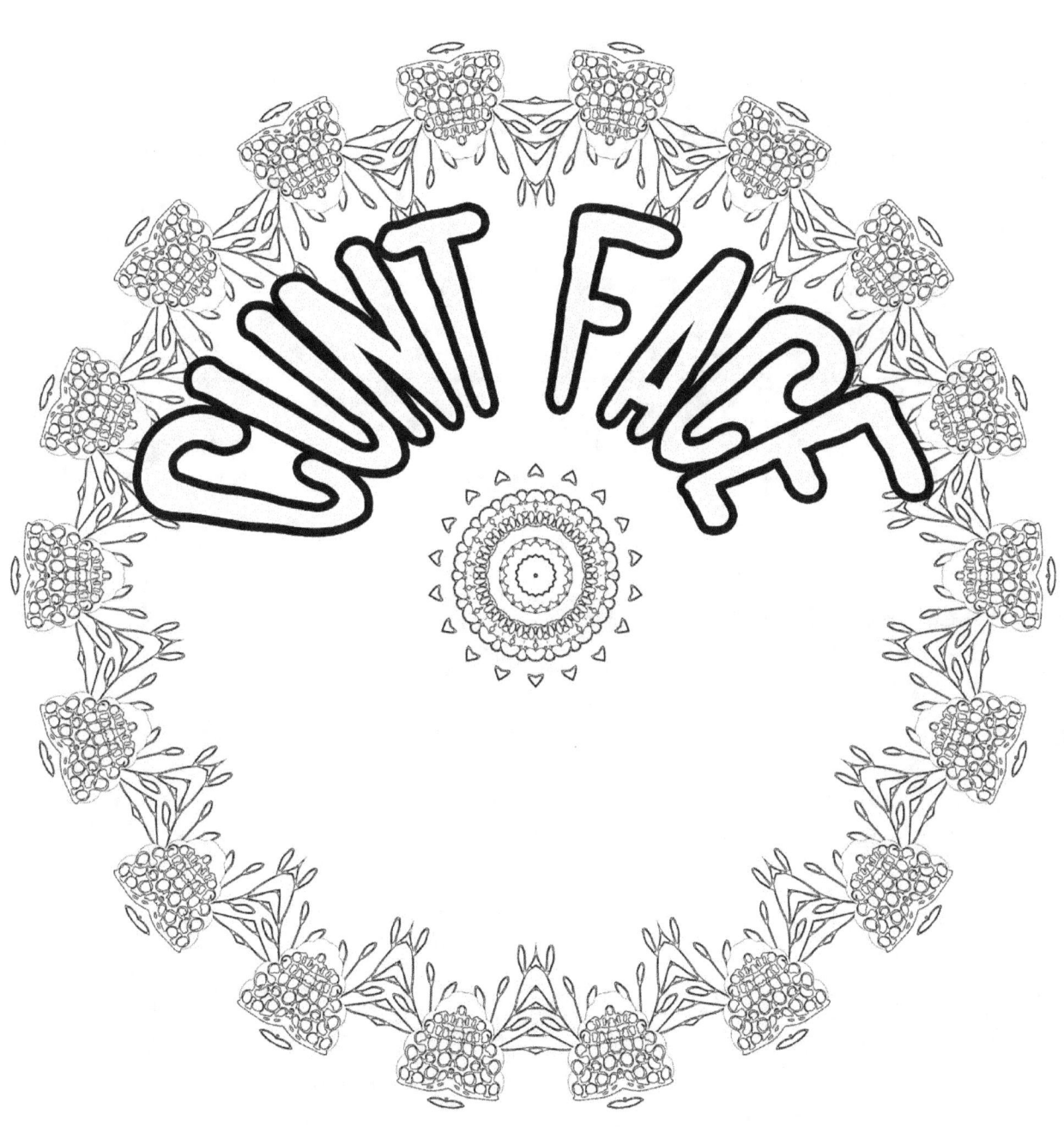

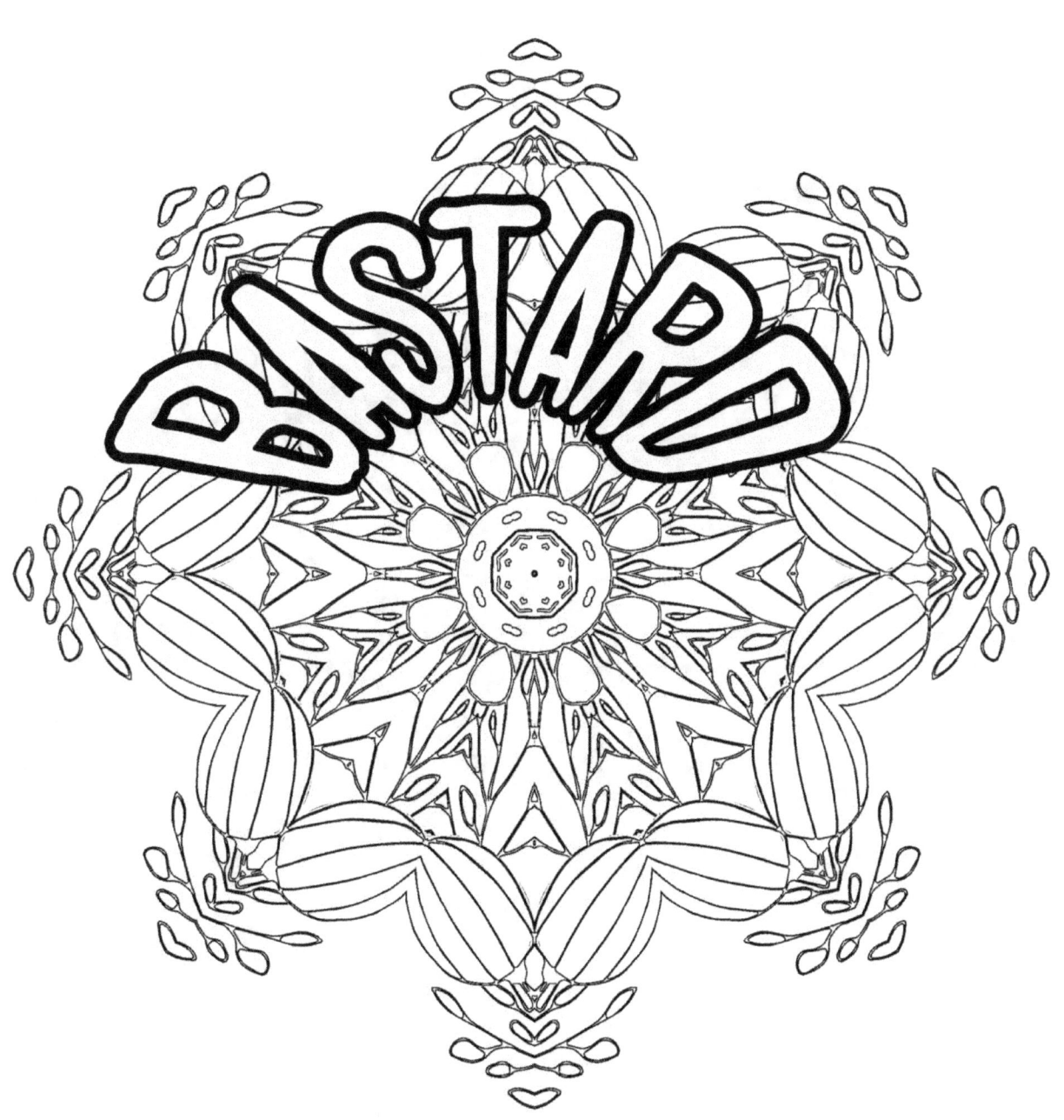

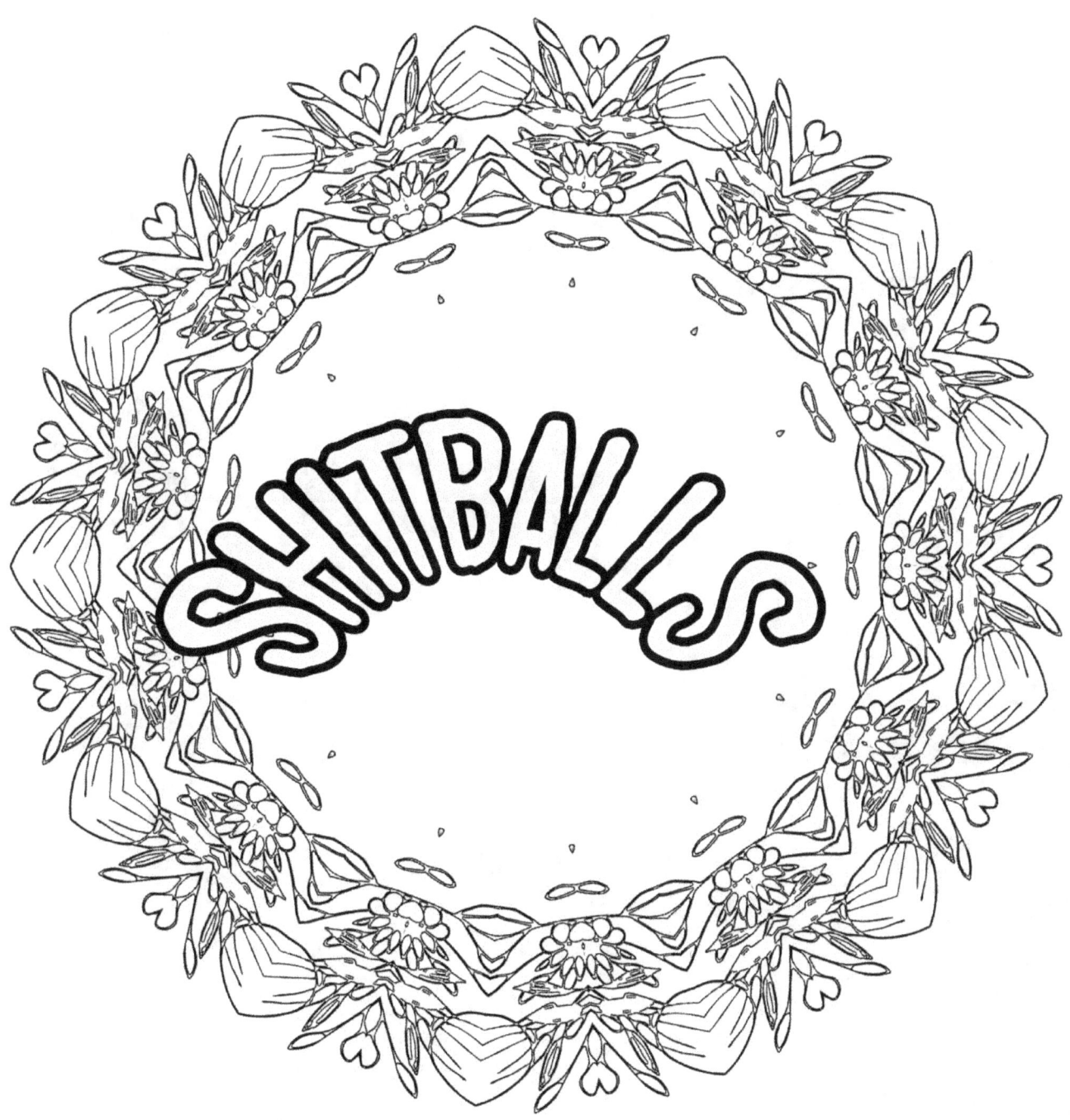

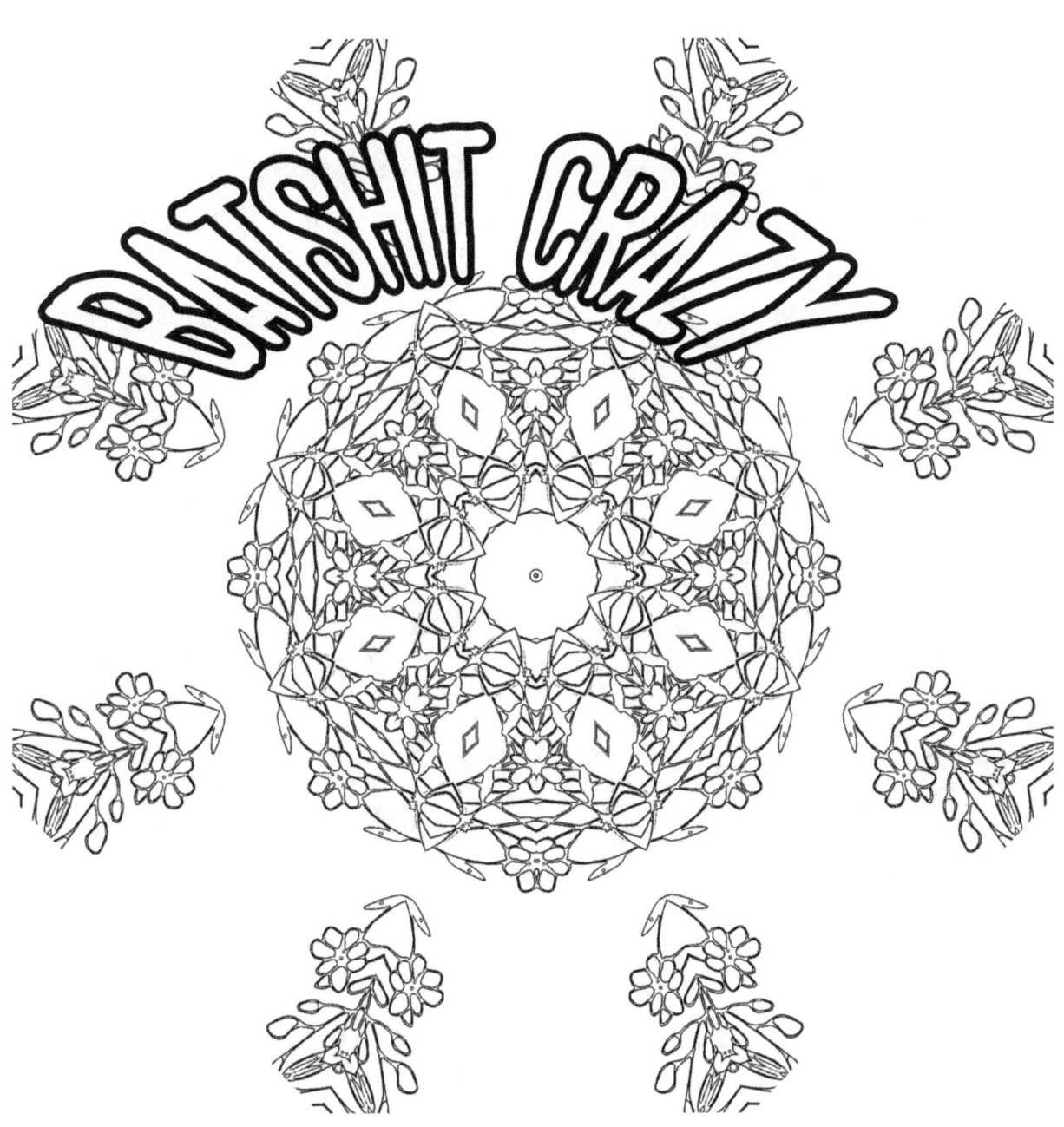

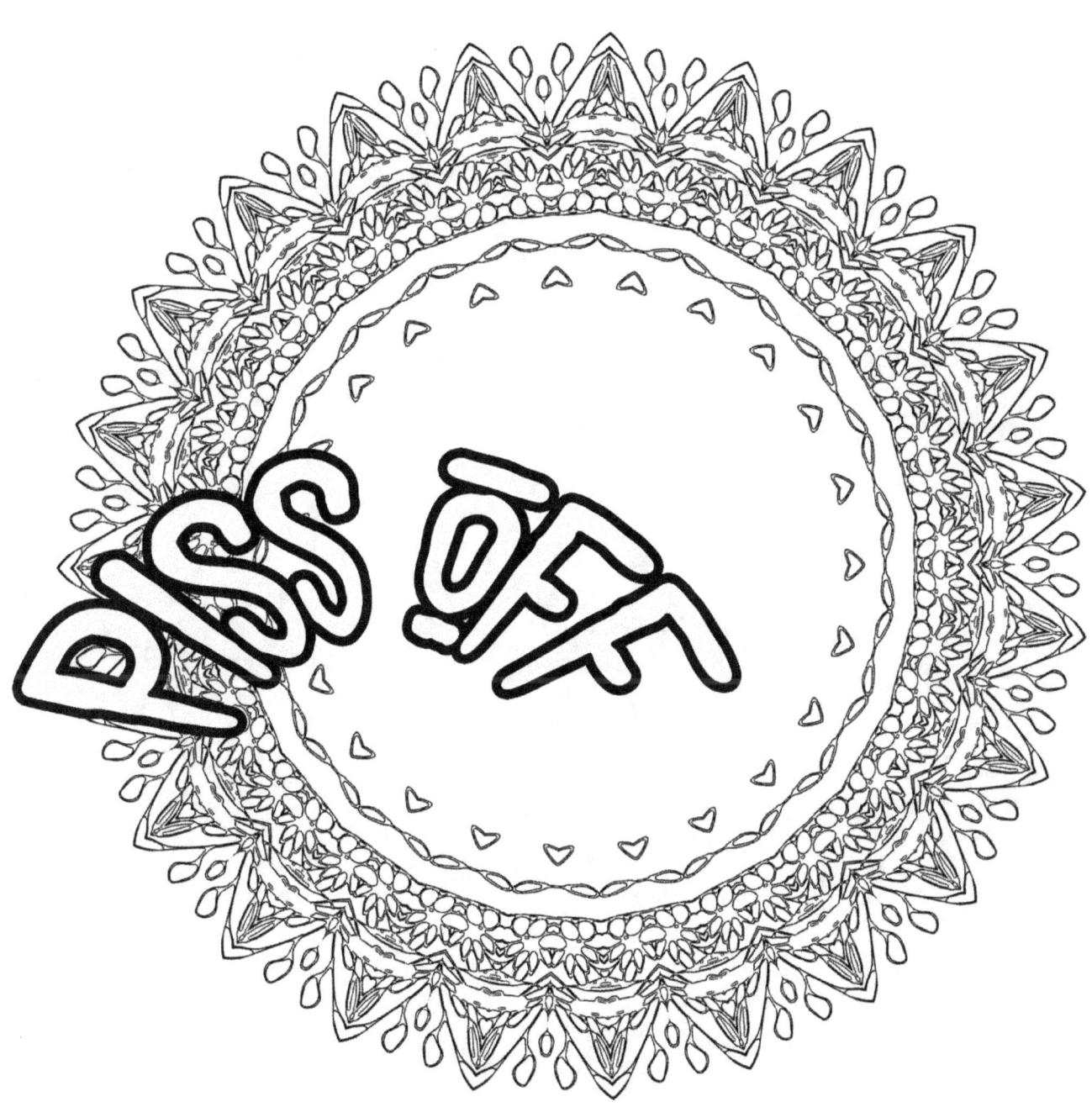

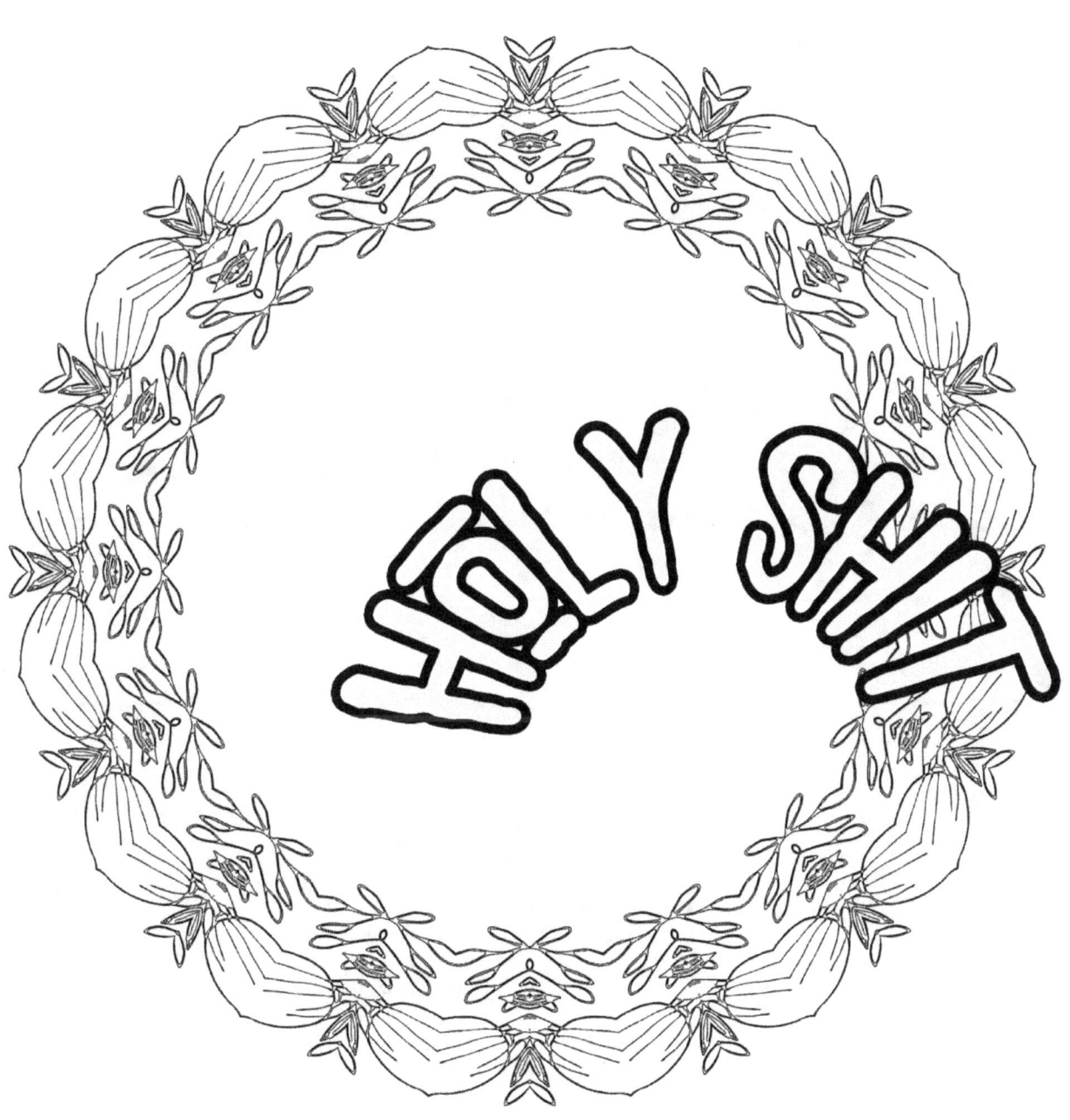

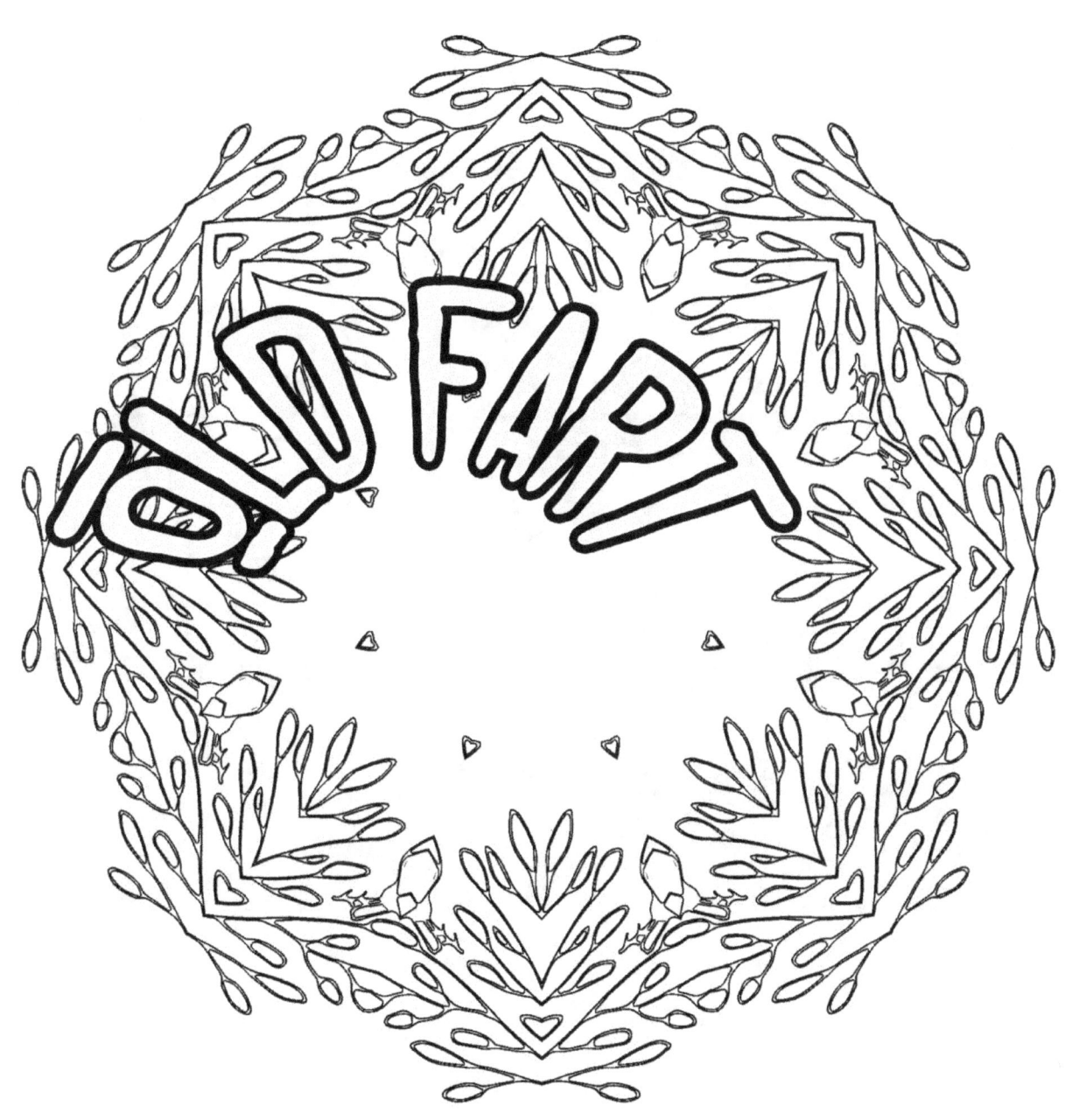

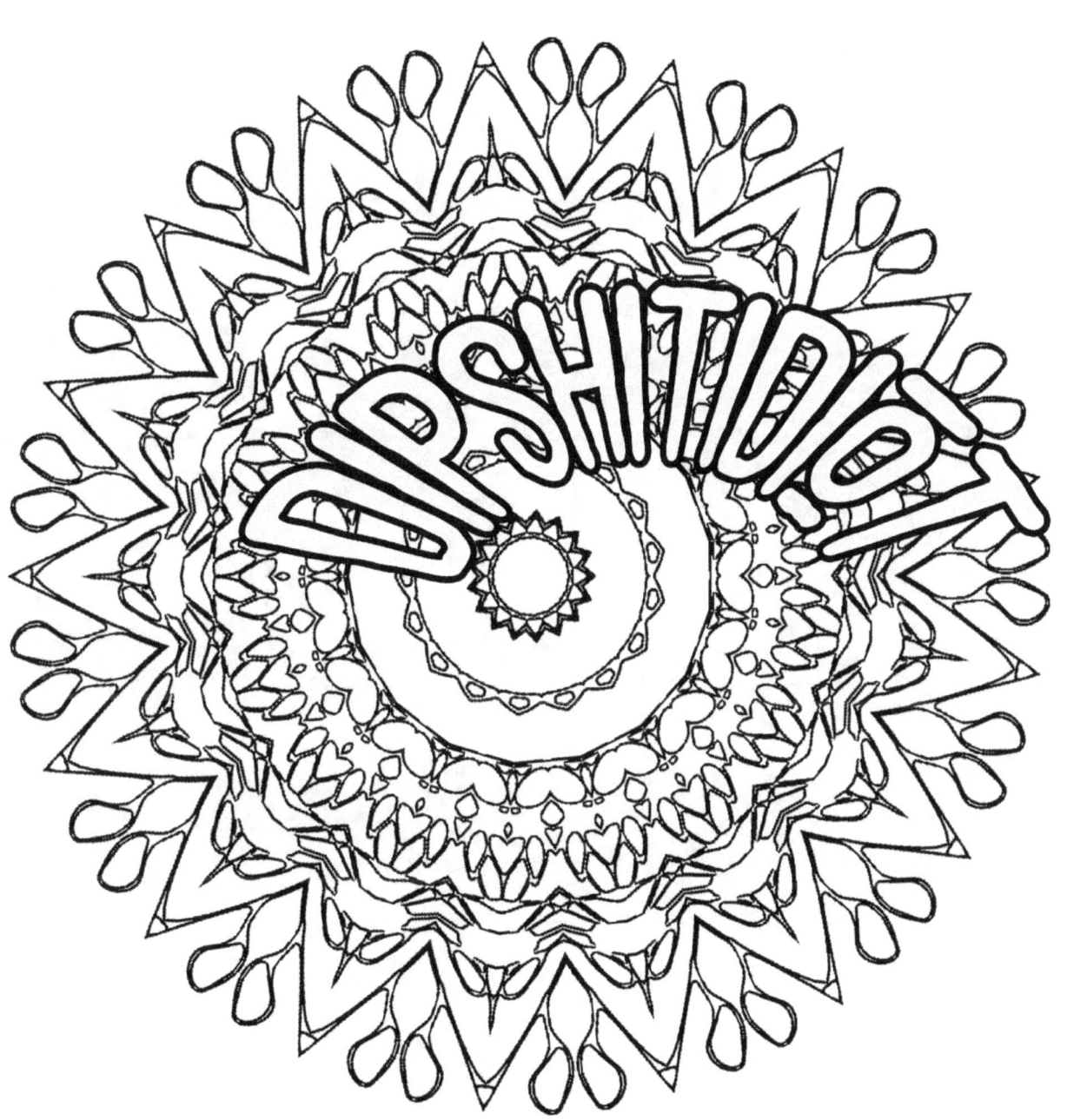

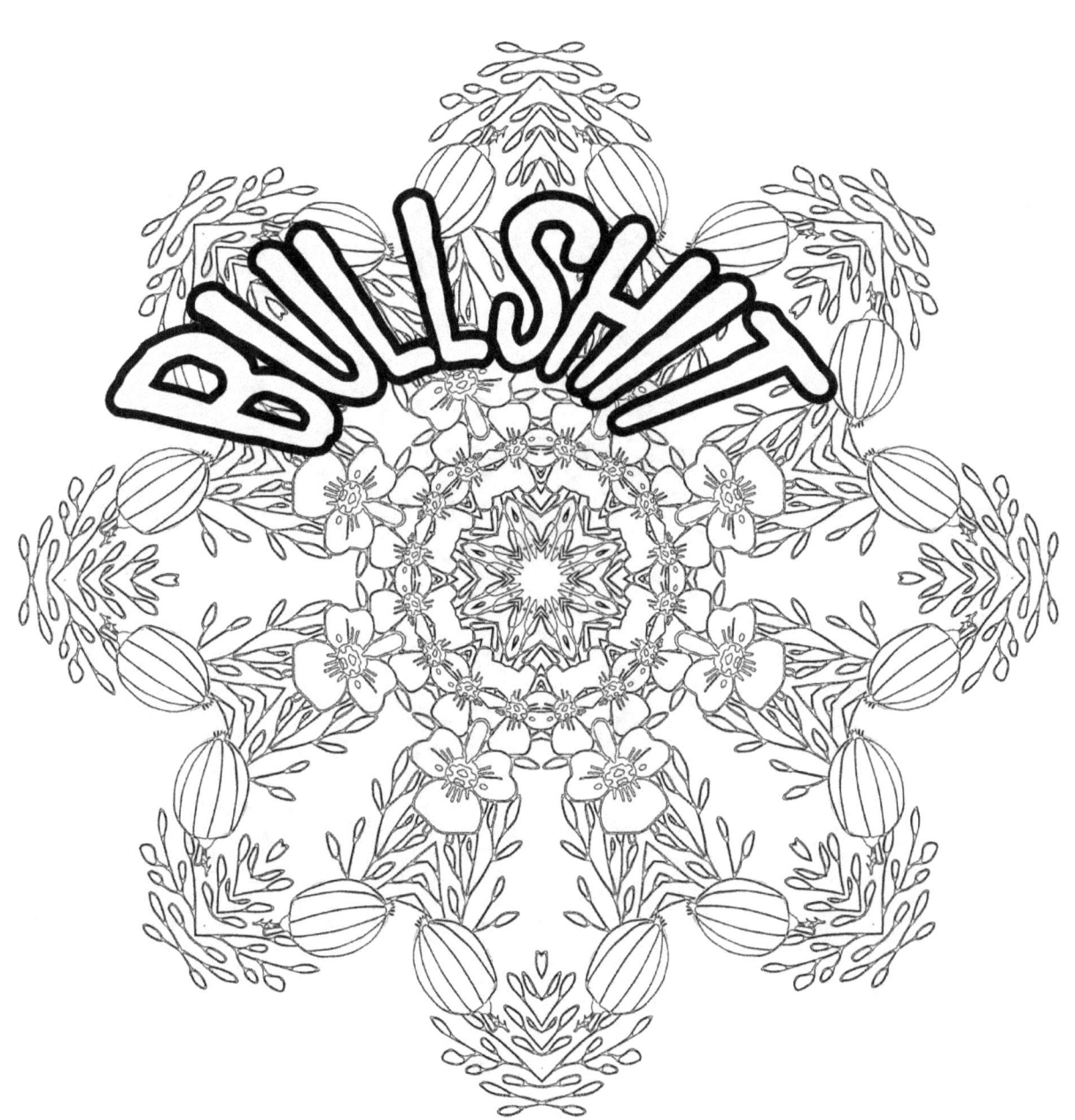

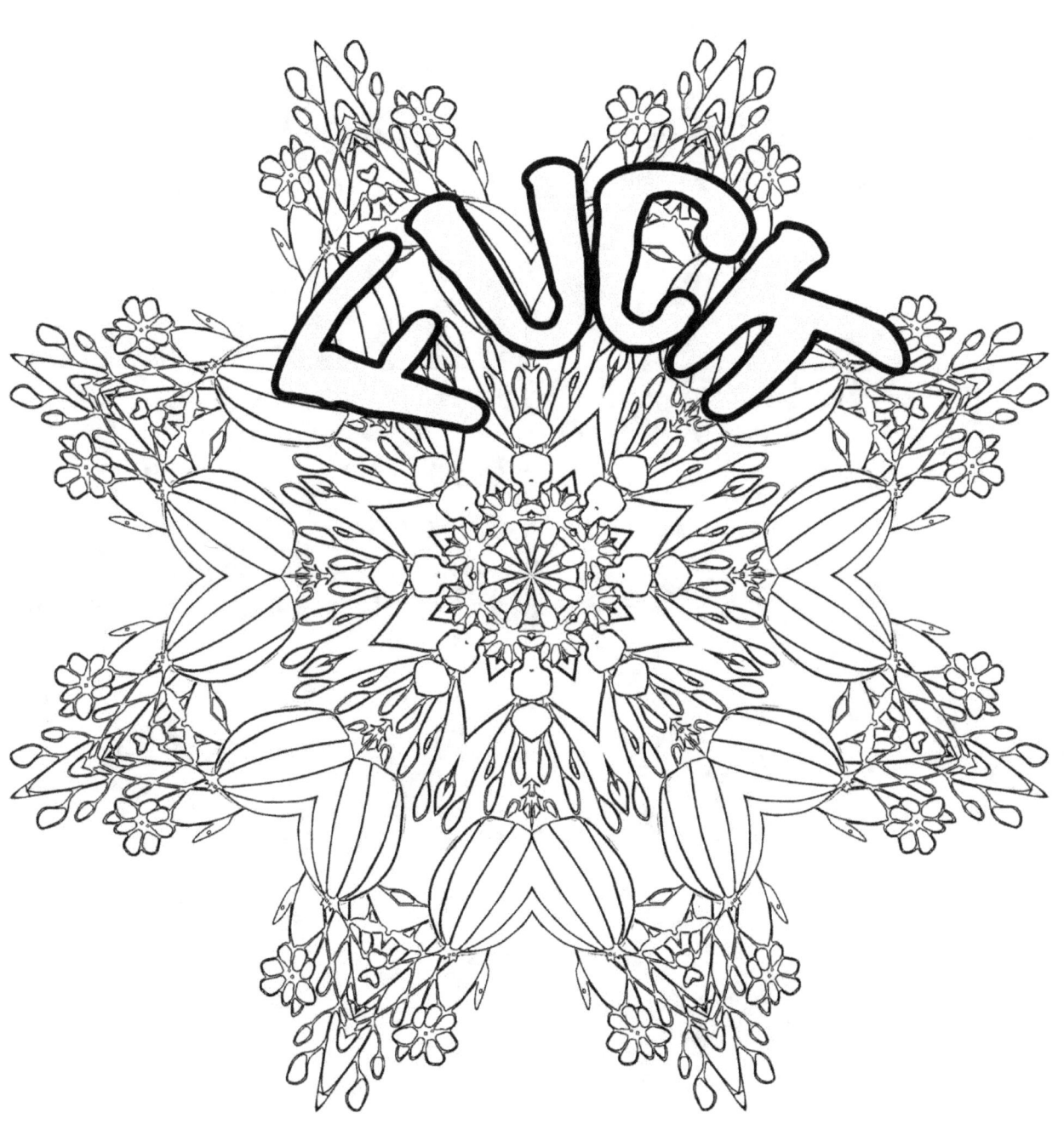

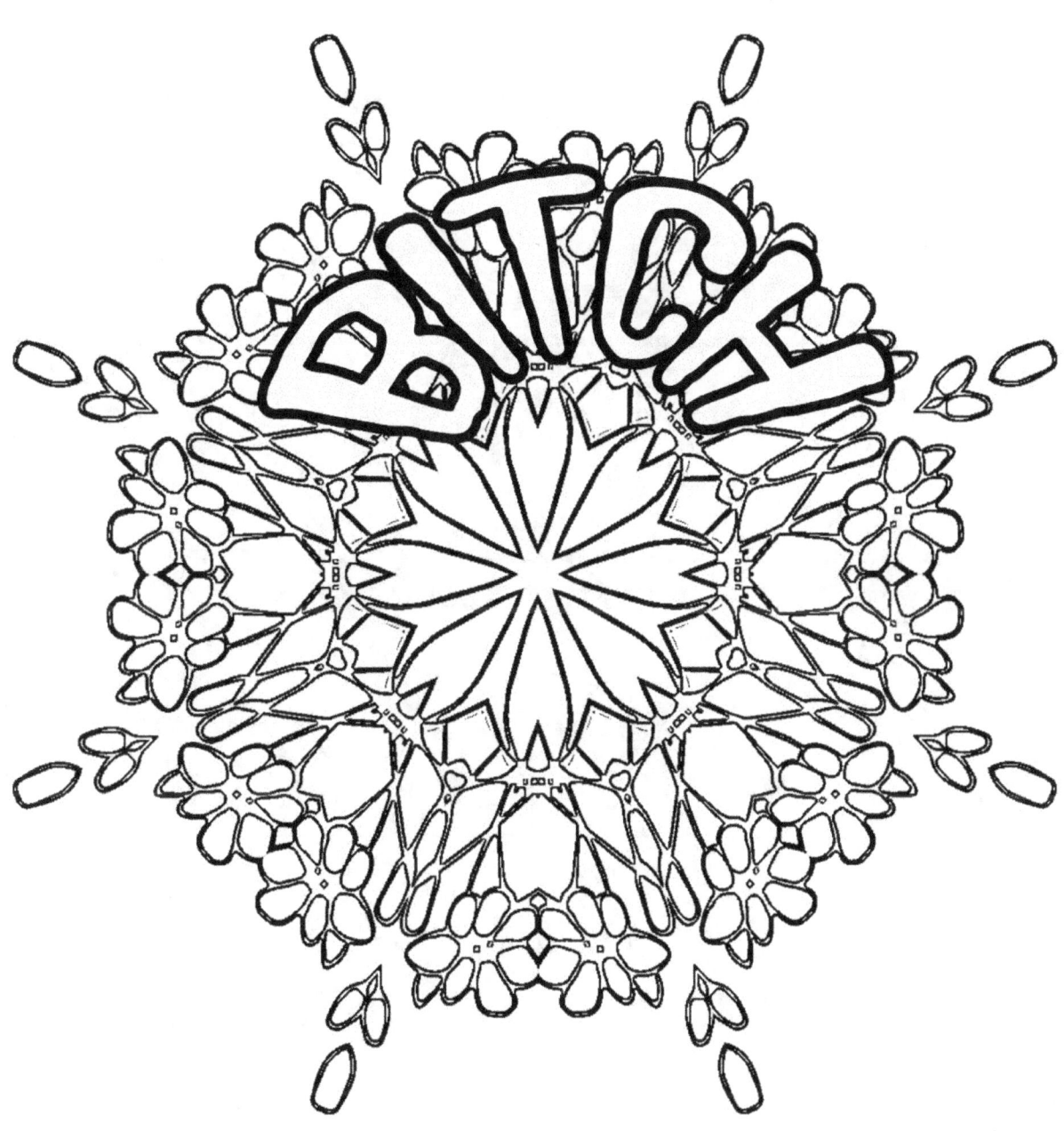

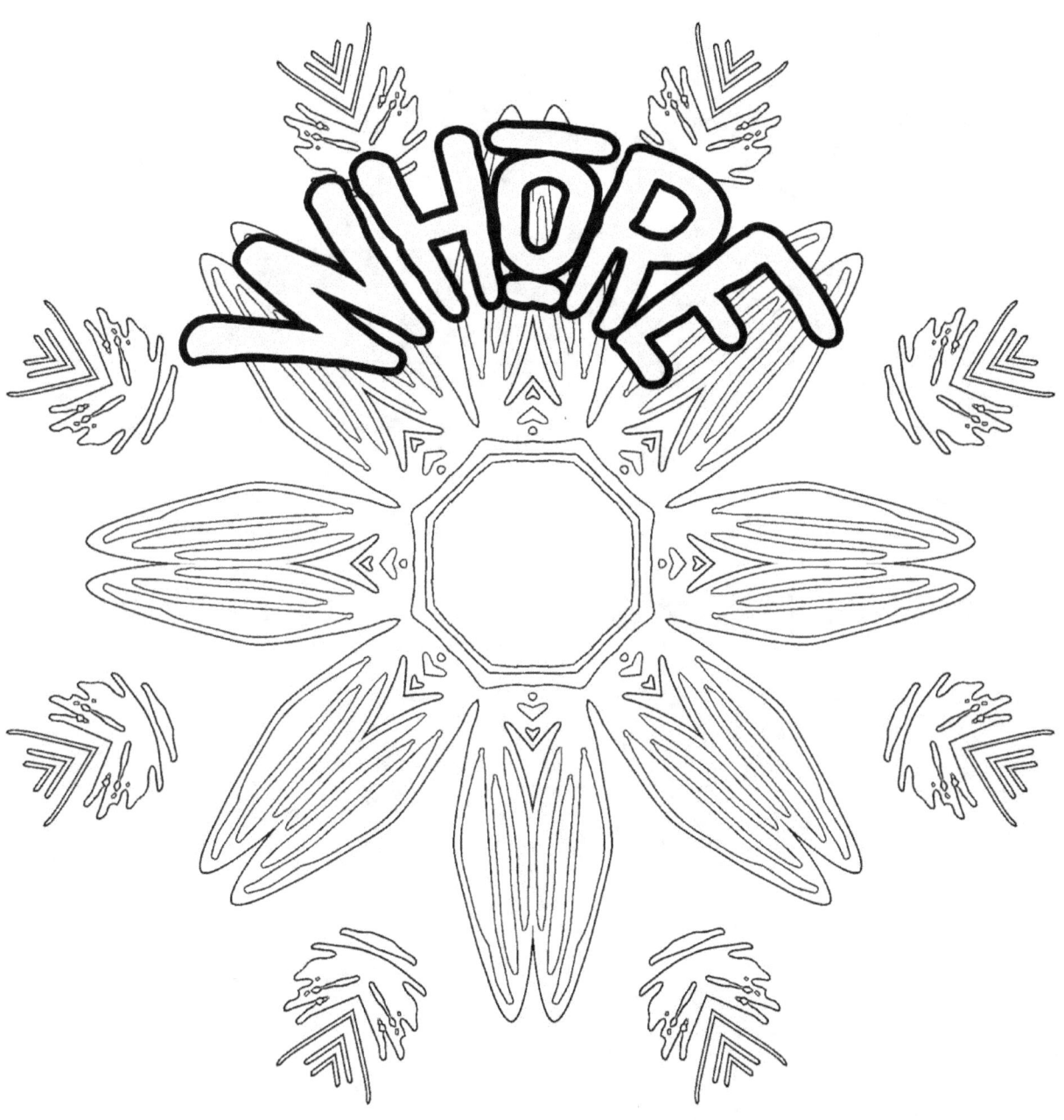

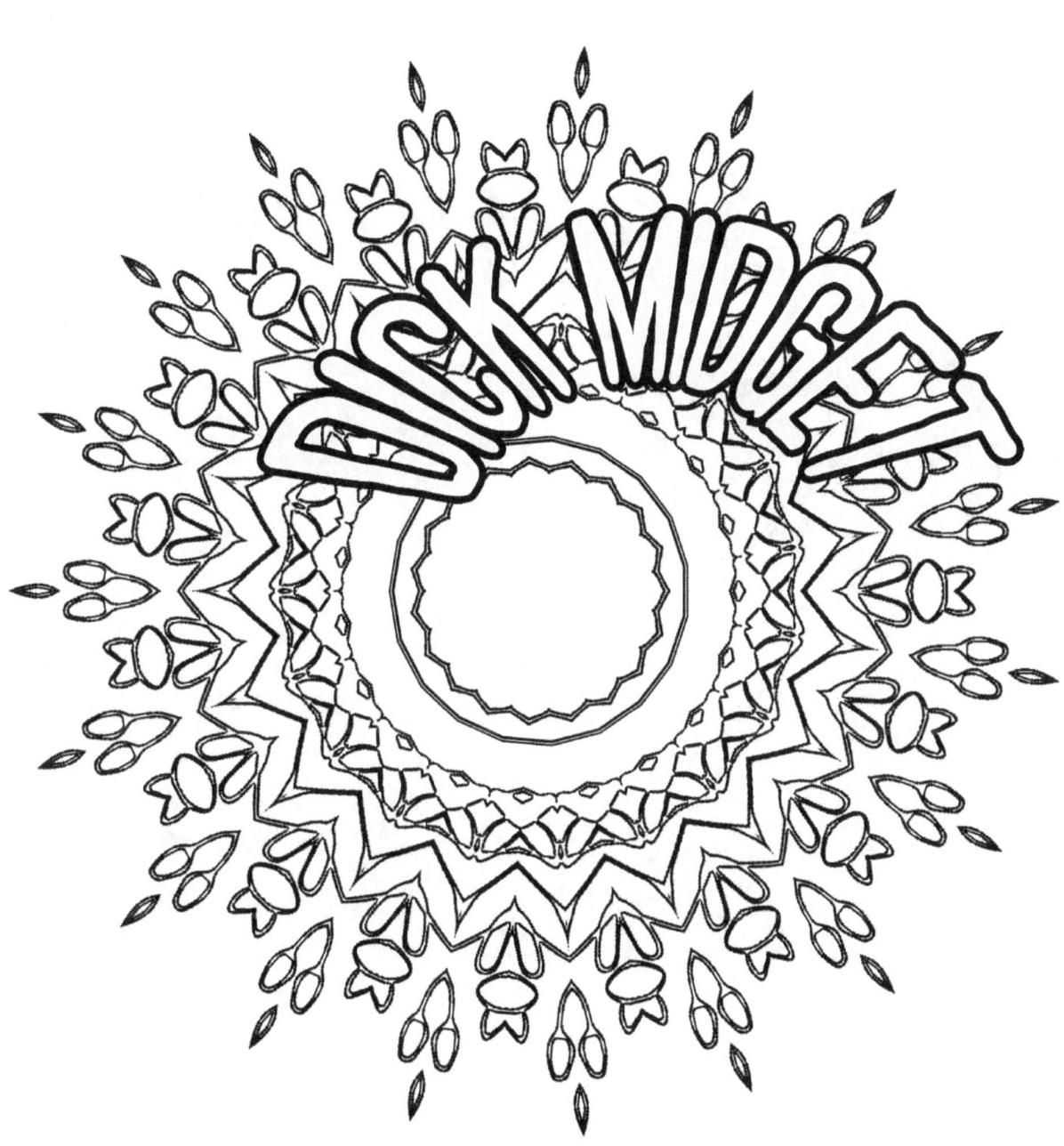

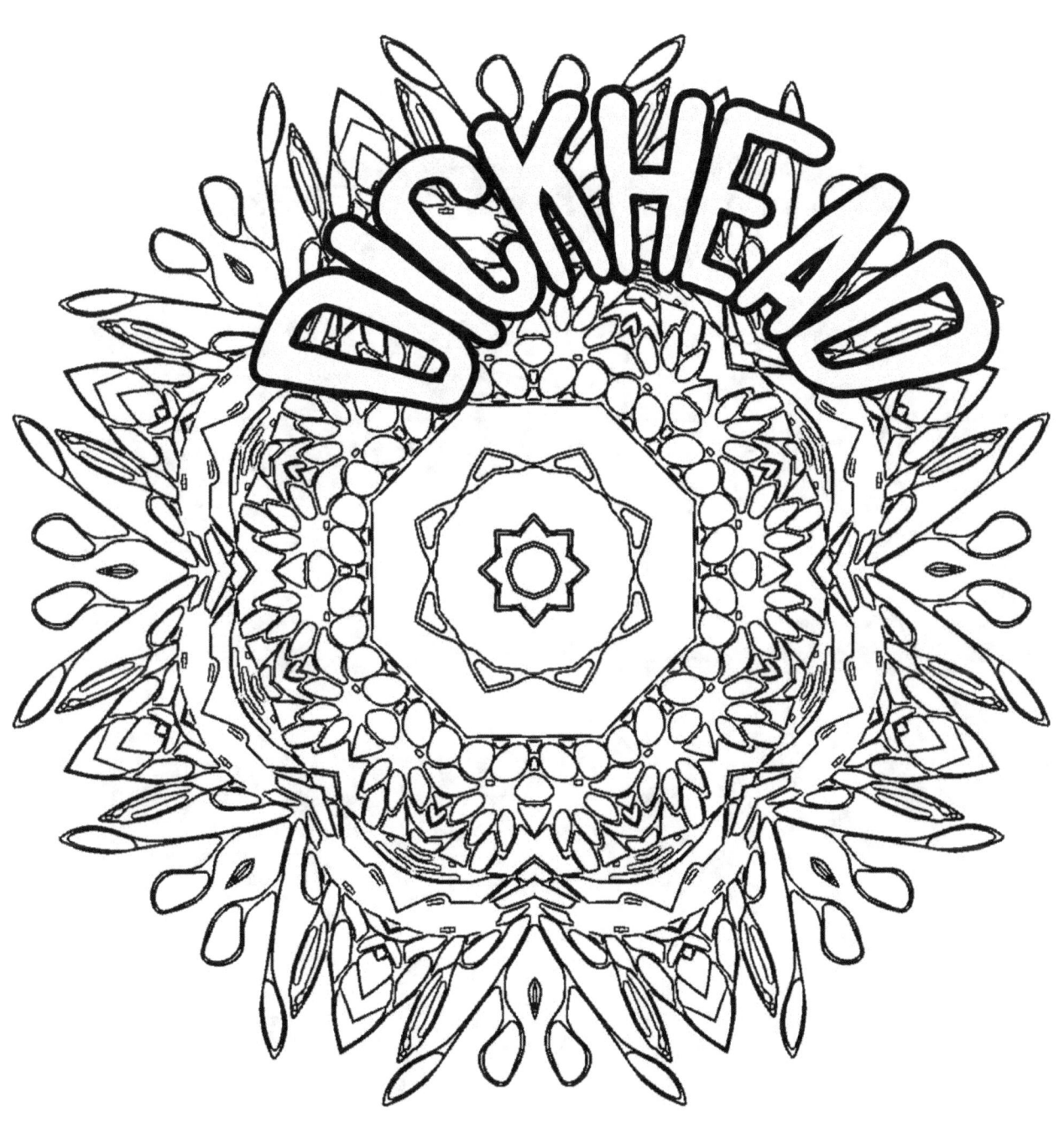

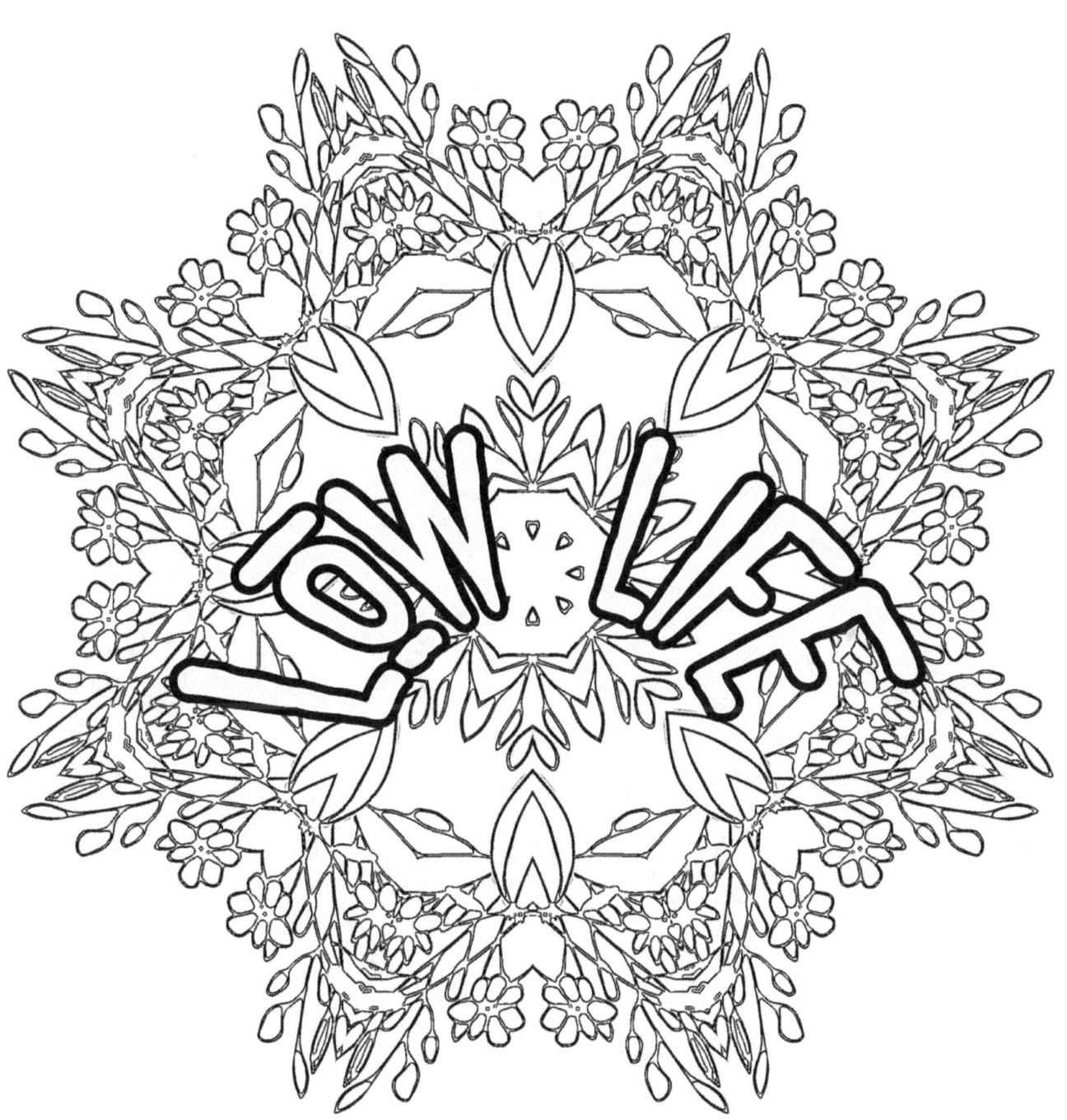

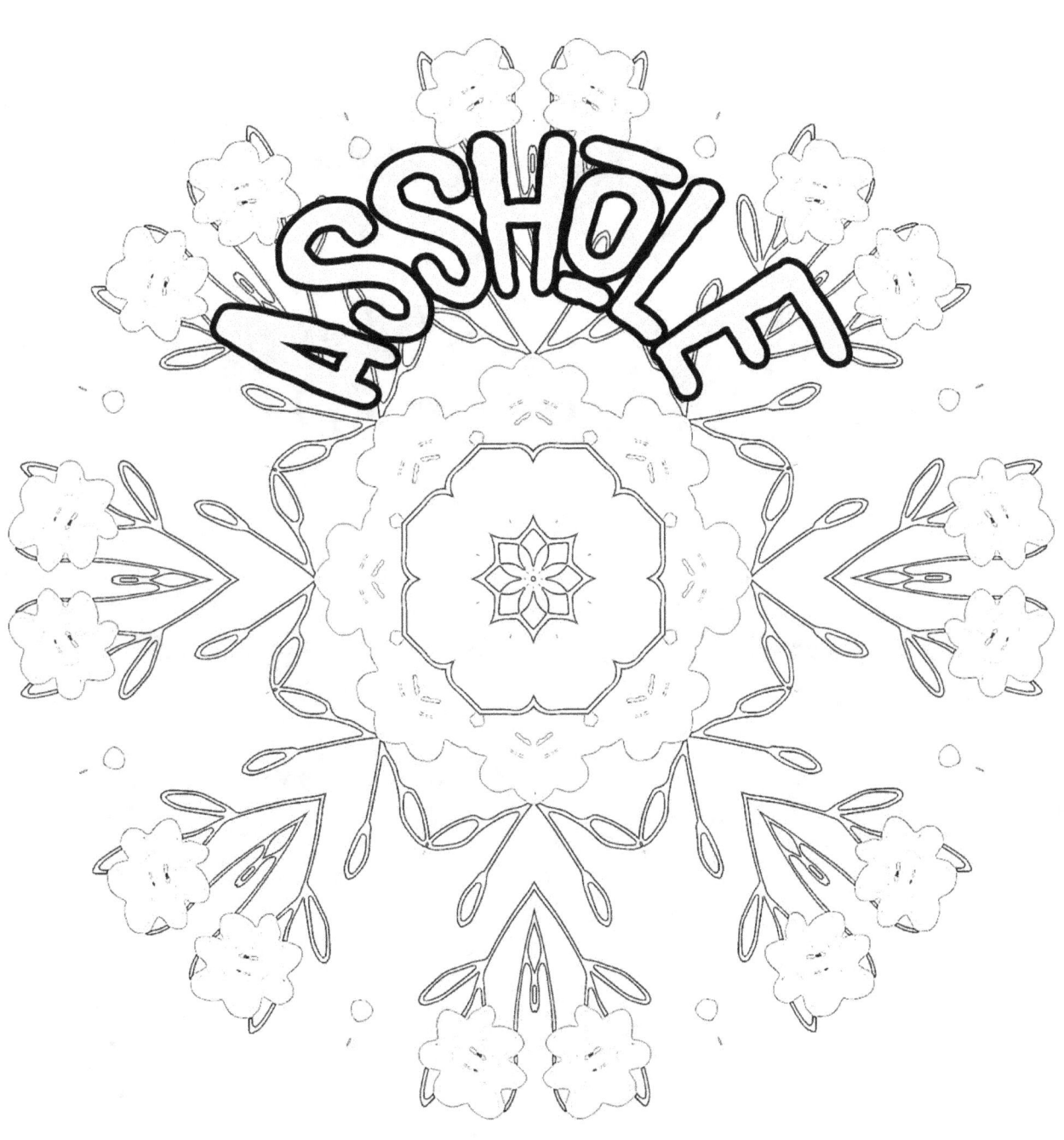

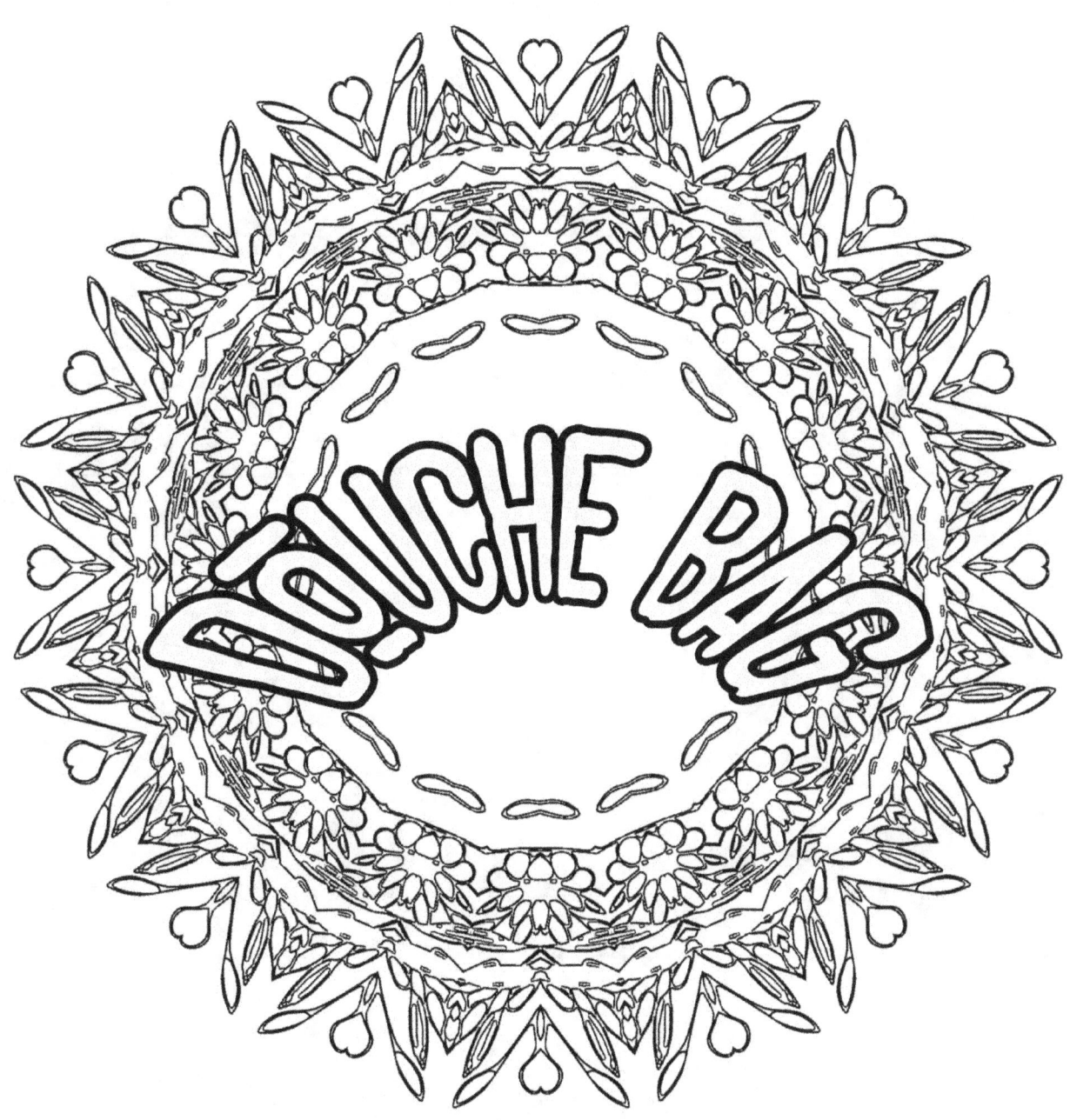

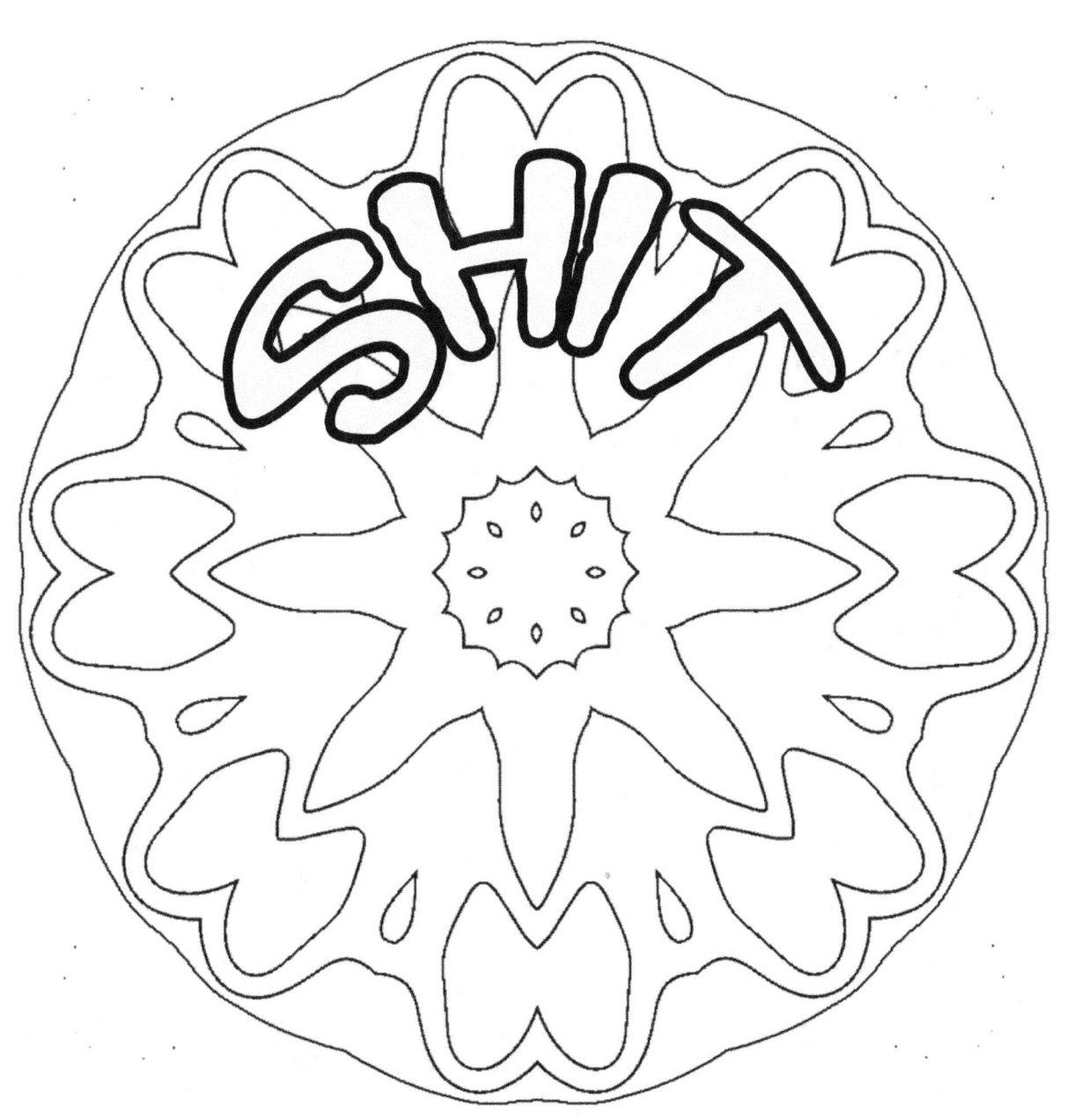

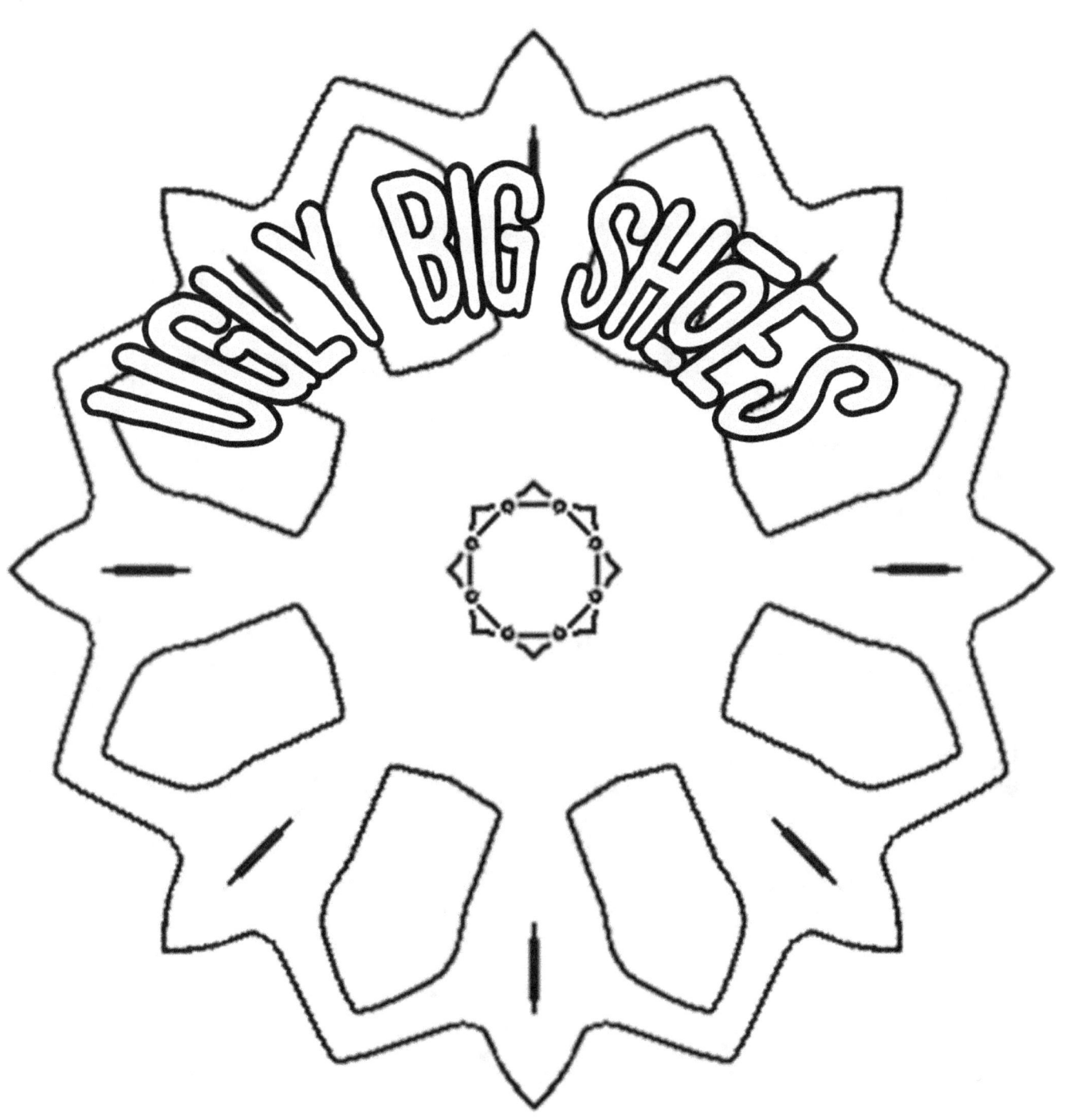

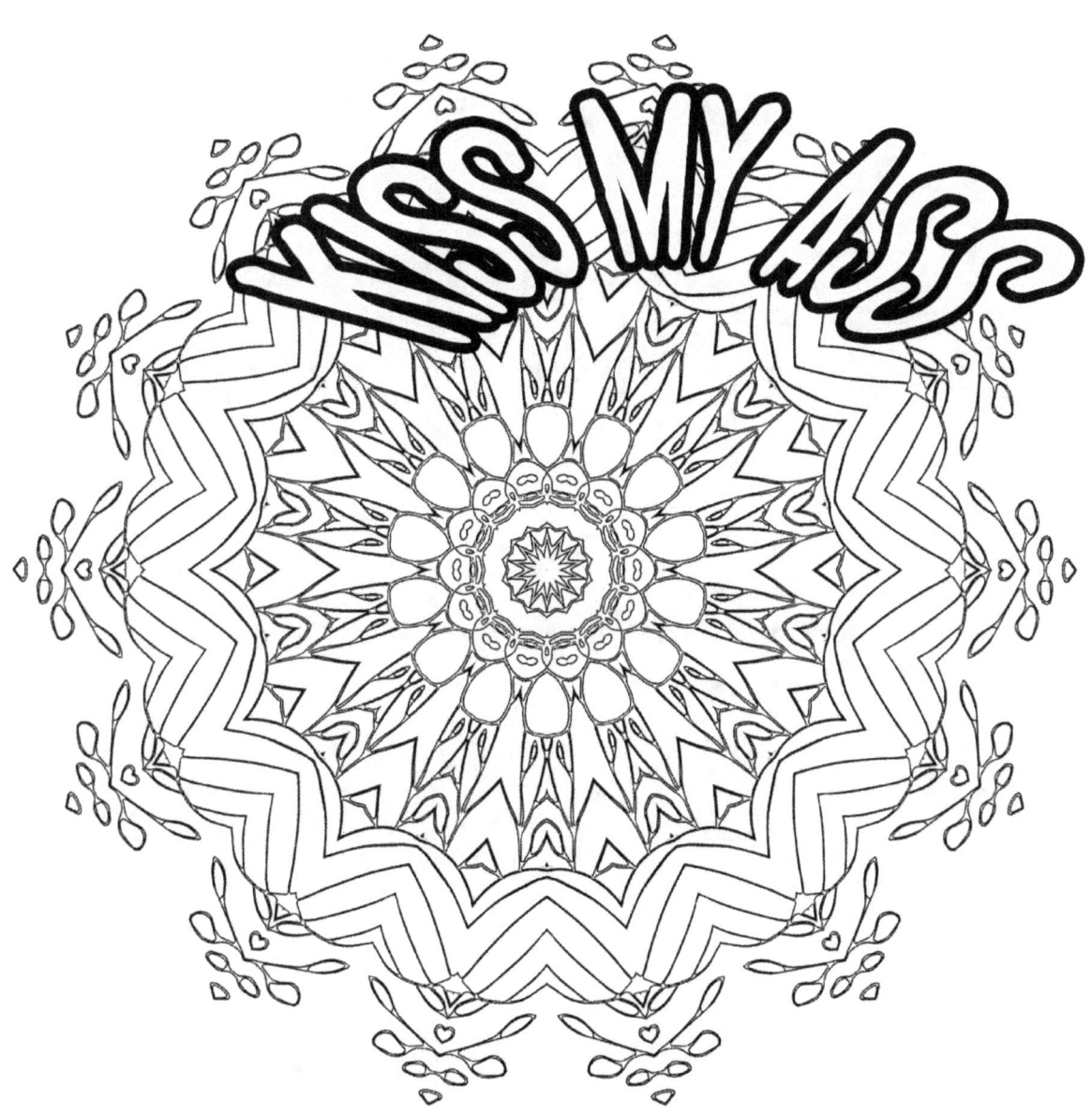

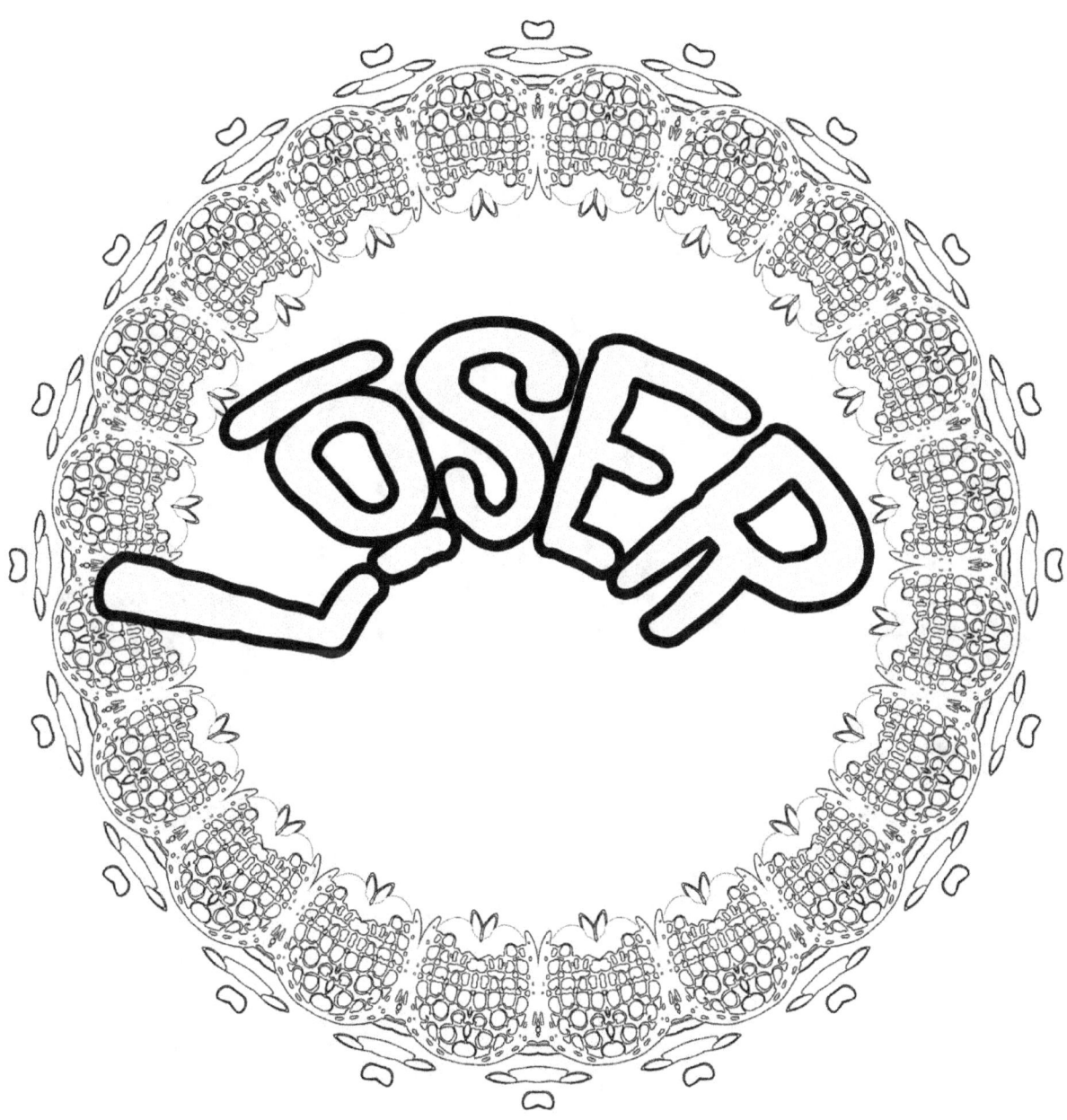

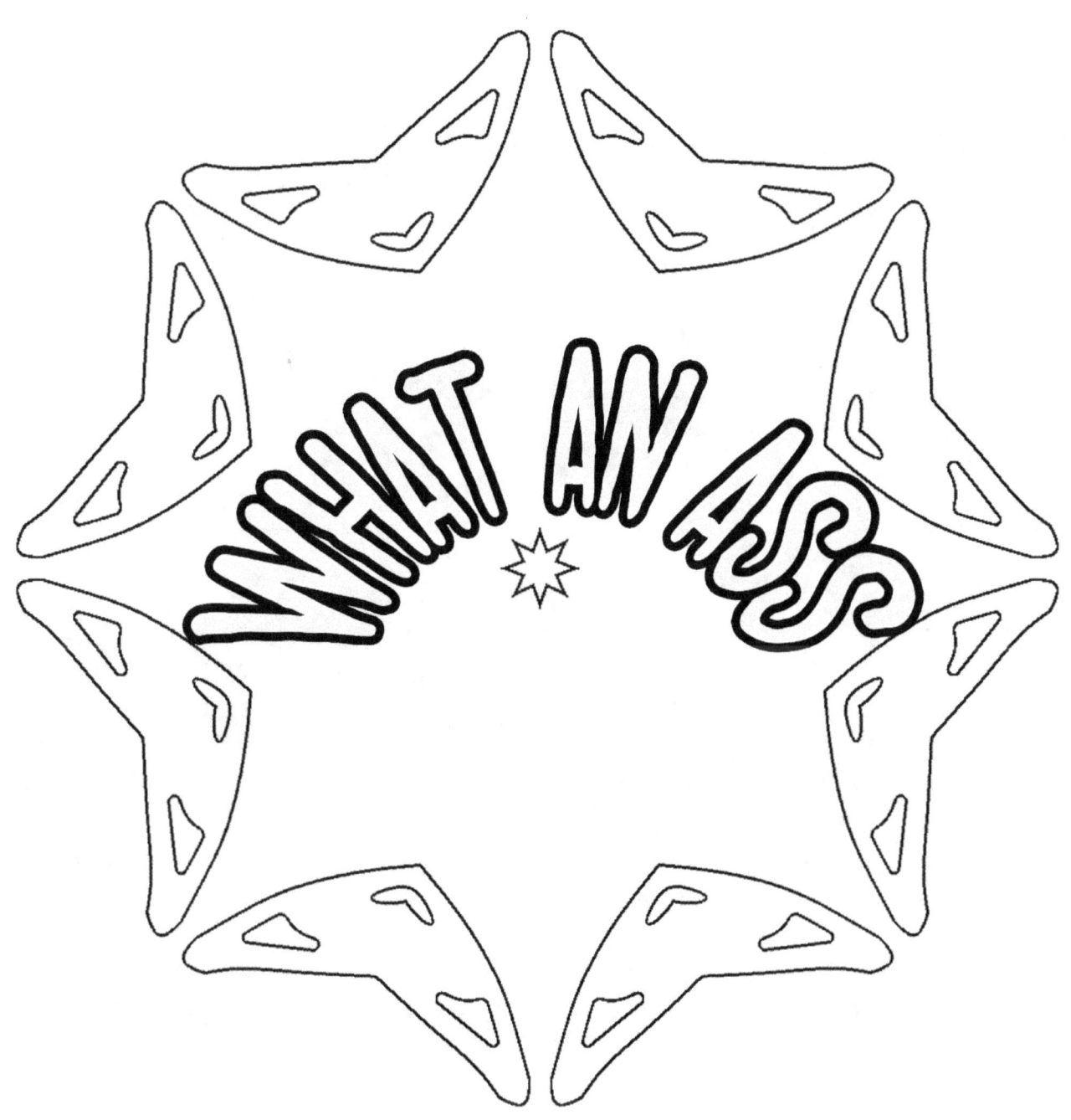

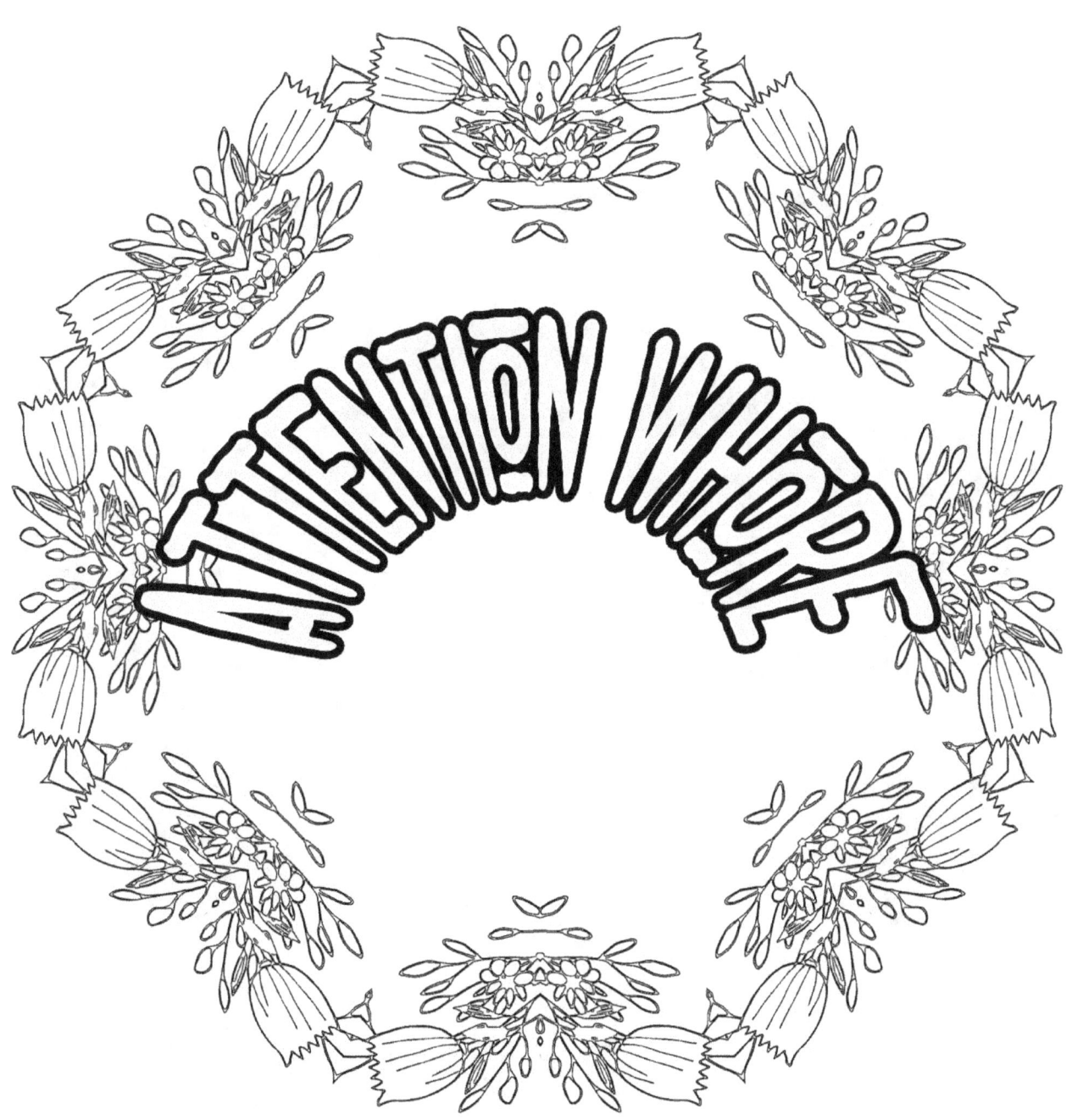

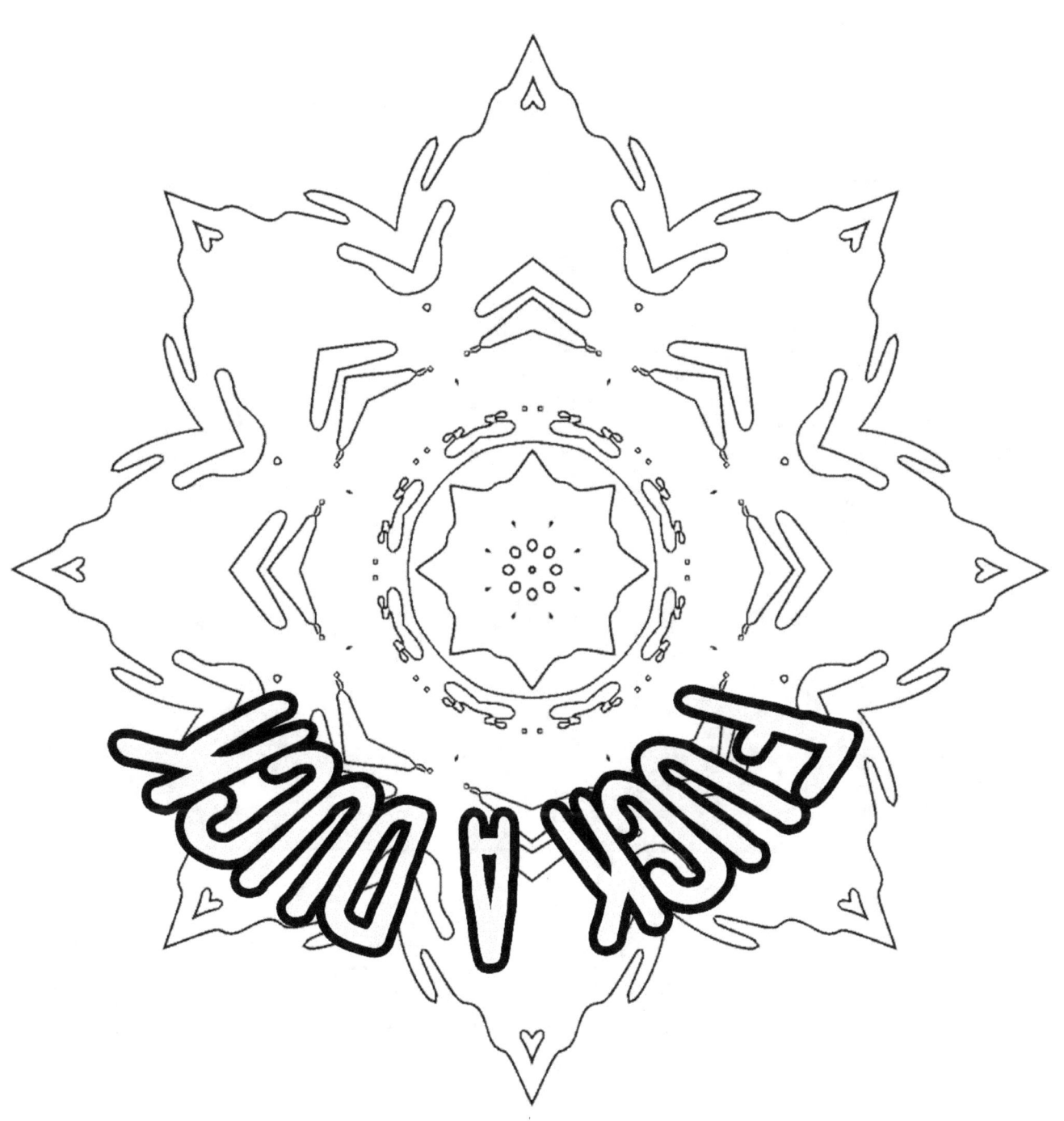

www.ingramcontent.com/pod-product-compliance
Lightning Source LLC
Chambersburg PA
CBHW081751170526
45167CB00009B/3993